"Ken Blanchard and Margret McBride have created a simple yet powerful little book that helps us all bridge the gap between the 'shoulda dones' and the 'dids' of day-to-day life. A quantum leap into compassion. You'll feel better for it."

—Kenny Loggins

"This marvelous book makes a compelling case for having one of the fiercest conversations known to man: an effective, heartfelt apology. This is often the only right thing to do; and very often it's the only thing to do. This book shows us how."

—Susan Scott, author of *Fierce Conversations: Achieving Success at Work & in Life, One Conversation at a Time*

"*The One Minute Apology* is an instant classic and a worthy companion to *The One Minute Manager*. It's must-reading and especially timely in the post-Enron business world."

—Sheldon Siegel, San Francisco attorney and bestselling author of *Criminal Intent* and *Special Circumstances*

"A quick, enjoyable read that had the power to accomplish a lasting and profound personal transformation. It's a message that will resonate from the boardroom to the mail room."

—Roger Gittines, coauthor of *Managing Up* and *Don't Fire Them, Fire Them Up!*

The One Minute Apology™

The One Minute Apology™

A Powerful Way To Make Things Better

**Ken Blanchard
and Margret McBride**

HarperCollinsPublishers

Grateful acknowledgment is made for permission to reprint the following:
Excerpt from chapter 23, "The Draft-Decision-Pathos" in *Abraham Lincoln:
The War Years*, volume III, Sangamon Edition by Carl Sandburg,
copyright 1939 by Harcourt, Inc., and renewed 1967 by Carl Sandburg,
reprinted by permission of Harcourt, Inc.

HarperCollins*Publishers*
77–85 Fulham Palace Road,
Hammersmith, London W6 8JB

www.**fire**and**water**.com

Published by HarperCollins*Publishers* 2003
1 3 5 7 9 8 6 4 2

A catalogue record for this book
is available from the British Library

ISBN 0 00 715923 4

Set in New Caledonia

Printed and bound in Great Britain by
Clays Ltd, St Ives plc

To all of us who could have made life better at work and at home with a few well-timed and sincere delivered apologies

Contents

Foreword

Spencer Johnson, M.D.

The One Minute Apology is the story of a corporate leader who, in the middle of these changing times, has made the kind of mistake we see all too often in the headlines of our newspapers.

It is easy to wonder how such smart and apparently successful people can get so far off track and lose sight of what's really important. Then, all too often, we see them compound their mistake by not acknowledging that they are wrong and not apologizing for what they have done in a way that makes good sense—by changing their behavior.

And of course if we watch the real-life drama unfold, the situation, uncorrected, usually gets worse. Yet how many of us can see ourselves in these stories—even though we may not have similar positions or have made similar mistakes? We have all invariably made mistakes of our own.

In the story that follows, you can discover what you can do in your own business or life to recognize when you have been wrong and to apologize to the people you harmed in a way that can make a bad situation into a better one.

Few things are more powerful than having the common sense, wisdom, and strength to admit when you've made a mistake and to set things right.

Ken Blanchard and Margret McBride show us a great way to deal with our mistakes successfully through the eyes of a young man who learns the secrets of a meaningful apology.

In the opening chapter, we see the company president's dilemma. Then the young man goes to The One Minute Manager's summer lake home, where he gains important insights into how he can help.

The young man's journey brings us to our own discoveries about what we can do to make things better, at work or at home, with our own one minute apologies.

If our leaders used the One Minute Apology to make needed changes, our world would be a better place to live in. But why wait? We can use the One Minute Apology ourselves to improve our *own* world and enjoy the tremendous results.

The One Minute Apology is more than a technique. And it is certainly more than just words. It is a useful way to think and live more successfully.

I hope you enjoy reading the story and benefiting from it as much as I have.

The Journey

Once there was a bright young man who set out on a life-changing journey. A major crisis at the company where he worked troubled him greatly and sent him on his quest. Little did he know that he would soon discover a secret power that was known to only a few, but would be valued by many.

The Company President

It was a Friday before a three-day holiday weekend and an emergency meeting of the board of directors was in progress. In the company's boardroom the president was speaking from the head of a long table.

At first the president spoke confidently as he began to describe the nature of the problem, but his tone changed after he was asked a few questions. *"How long has this been going on? When was the first time you learned of this? Why didn't you take action before now? Couldn't you have seen what the consequences of such actions might be?"*

Refusing to take responsibility, the president became defensive and combative, and this made things worse.

The board members had never heard the president talk like this. When he stopped, silence filled the room. Everyone was stunned by what had just happened.

The Young Man

As a chief assistant to the president, the young man sat in on many board meetings at the president's request, but he'd never seen one like this. It came as a shock because the young man admired the president. The older man helped him recognize his potential and had given him his first big opportunity after business school.

What would happen now?

Is this the beginning of the end? the young man thought, feeling his heart sink. *How will our company survive?*

He knew that the president needed to take a new course of action, or every employee's position would be in jeopardy. Indeed, even the future of the company was at stake.

The young man listened as the chairman of the board addressed the president.

"Well, we've heard all of your excuses and rationalizations," the chairman began. "Frankly, I am unimpressed. If we don't resolve this quickly, our company's reputation in the marketplace will be ruined along with its stock value."

"On Tuesday morning, after the holiday weekend," the chairman continued, "we will meet here again. You deserve an opportunity to set the record straight. Between now and then think carefully about what you plan to say and do. If you haven't come up with an effective way to restore our confidence, we may have to look for new leadership."

The chairman called for adjournment. Obviously shaken, the president stood up to leave the room.

The young man opened the boardroom door. As the president strode past, he signaled for the young man to follow him to his waiting car.

"Please leave word on my voice mail where you are going to be this weekend in case I need to reach you," the president said. "If possible, I would like you to join me in my office at 7:00 A.M. Monday to prepare for Tuesday's meeting."

As the car sped away, a sense of dread came over the young man. He knew the president was making a big mistake. Everyone on the board seemed to see it except the president himself. The young man thought, *What can I do to help?*

Back in his office, the young man pondered the situation. What could the president possibly say to the board of directors Tuesday morning to avoid his downfall? *Where can I find the answers that might help him set things right?*

Then he remembered what his late father had told him: "If you ever need help, call my friend the One Minute Manager. He'll always be happy to help you."

The young man called the One Minute Manager's office and learned that he was vacationing at his lake house with his wife Carol and their kids Annie and Brad. Hearing that brought back many happy memories of when he and his parents visited them every summer. Brad and Annie were almost like a brother and sister to him. It had been five years since his last visit there.

The young man left a message on the One Minute Manager's voice mail summarizing his problem. He said he needed expert advice by Monday at the latest, but certainly understood if the One Minute Manager didn't want to interrupt his vacation with his family.

The One Minute Manager

Later at his apartment, the young man's telephone rang. He immediately picked it up, and heard the One Minute Manager's powerful, positive voice, "Of course, I'd love to help you! *There is a powerful secret that I've taught many people, and once they begin to use it effectively, they are able to solve problems more easily. It's called the One Minute Apology.* It sounds like this is what your president needs."

"*One Minute Apology?*" the young man asked.

"It's more than I can cover in this phone call. Join us at the lake for the weekend! You'll see your problem from a new perspective. You might also want to bring your golf clubs. We'll have fun as we problem solve! There's a flight at 7:30 this evening. Brad can meet you at the airport when you land. Annie arrives tomorrow morning. They're going to be excited to see you again! And they are experts on the One Minute Apology."

The young man's spirits lifted as he decided to go.

"Regarding the One Minute Apology," said the One Minute Manager, "on your way here you might give this some thought:

✷

The Toughest Part
Of Apologizing
Is Realizing
And
Admitting
That
You Were Wrong

✷

The One Minute Apology

On the way to the airport, the young man called the president's voice mail, left word where he could be reached and confirmed their meeting early Monday morning. Hearing the president's voice on voice mail heightened the young man's anxiety over the situation at work.

After the young man's flight landed, Brad met him at baggage claim. They gave each other a warm hug. It was as if they had just seen each other yesterday. They talked the whole way home. When they arrived at the lake, the One Minute Manager and his wife Carol greeted the young man warmly and told him how happy they were that he was back. As he walked through the living room, he noticed that little had changed. The cozy, comfortable furnishings invited a sense of relaxation.

The One Minute Manager offered the young man a cool drink. After catching up on each other's lives, Brad and Carol excused themselves to give the One Minute Manager and the young man time to talk privately.

The One Minute Manager got right to the point, "You are here for such a short time, let's set some goals about what you want to accomplish this weekend."

"My main goal is to get your advice about how I might help my president. Under different circumstances, I would love to play golf with you, but getting a handle on this problem could take all weekend.

"If only things could have gone differently . . . maybe I should have . . ."

The One Minute Manager responded, "You will have time to play golf and solve your problem. But first, you need to stop using phrases like *should have, could have, would have,* and *if only.* Those are 'worry words.' They make you feel overwhelmed, discouraged, and confused. They keep you stuck in the past and prevent you from taking your best course of action. *They also keep you from being honest with yourself.*"

The young man looked puzzled.

The One Minute Manager said, "Do you want to look back on this weekend as time spent agonizing over things from the past that you can't change? Or do you want to remember it as the weekend you decided to learn new skills to make things better?"

"Of course, I'd prefer to learn how to make things better," answered the young man.

"Good," said the One Minute Manager as he got up and led the young man to the porch overlooking the lake.

The moon's reflection shimmered on the water's surface. In the distance, the pine trees and hills were silhouetted against the moon. They could see the flickering lights from the cabins across the lake.

The One Minute Manager sat down in one of the deck chairs and motioned for the young man to do the same. "Before we get started, let me share something important with you."

"Of course," the young man said.

"Do you know what appealed to me most about your voice mail?"

"No," answered the young man.

"You said you work for someone you admire, the company is in trouble, and you want to find a way to help. Do you know how rare that is? Many people say, 'That's not my worry.' They divorce themselves from the problem and steer clear of those involved. Psychologically, they jump ship. Then, once things blow over, they join back in. When someone like you cares enough to stay involved, I'll go to any length to help."

The young man responded, "Well, the president gave me a wonderful opportunity after I graduated, and mentors like that don't come along very often. I wouldn't feel very good about myself if I bailed out on him and the company now that they're both in trouble and may need help."

"I admire your attitude."

"Thank you," the young man said. "I also enjoy being part of a dynamic company and believe it is still possible for us to have a bright future. I also need to understand how things went so wrong, so fast. The whole situation is now such a mess. I hardly know where to begin."

As they sat on the porch, the young man described the problems at his company. When he finished, the One Minute Manager turned to him and said, "Given what you have just told me, I agree that this situation is more serious than I expected. I understand why you're concerned. If some well-thought-out action is not taken, your whole company could go down very quickly."

After a pause, the One Minute Manager continued, "The fact is, now I feel more strongly than ever that there is only *one* thing your president can do to make things dramatically better for everyone concerned."

"In your phone call you spoke about the One Minute Apology. Is that what you have in mind?" asked the young man.

"Absolutely. *Done properly, the One Minute Apology is one of the most powerful things anyone can do to repair a situation like the one you described.*"

"Then, please tell me all about it," replied the young man.

"For more than twenty years I have been using three management secrets," said the One Minute Manager.

"*I know,*" interjected the young man, "*One Minute Goal-Setting, Praisings, and Reprimands.*"

The One Minute Manager smiled, saying, "Shortly after I was asked to teach the three secrets to others, a top manager asked me, 'What happens when managers make mistakes. What can they do to get back on track?'

"That's when I started thinking about the One Minute Apology. Some people call it my fourth secret. All I know is that as soon as you realize you have made a mistake, you need to apologize."

The young man said in a reflective mood, "In this present situation my president has certainly made some serious mistakes. Will apologizing be enough?"

"Not if the apology is merely words," the One Minute Manager replied.

"So the real power of the One Minute Apology lies with actions, not words," said the young man.

When the Manager nodded in agreement, the young man opened his journal and wrote down:

*

*The Power Of
The One Minute Apology
Is Deeper Than
Just Words*

*

"There is more to apologizing than I realized," observed the young man.

"Mistakes fester and poison relationships," the One Minute Manager continued. *"No matter what else is going right, if your president doesn't admit his mistakes right away and then deal with them by changing his behavior, he will lose the confidence of the board, and careers and relationships will be damaged."*

"So apologizing has the potential to not only correct a wrong, but restore the confidence others have in you."

"That's why an obvious change in behavior is so important," said the One Minute Manager. *"In a One Minute Apology you admit you are wrong and you deal with the cause of the damage instead of the symptoms."*

"It's hard to believe you can do all of that in a minute," remarked the young man.

"It's called the One Minute Apology because in most cases it can be said in a minute, even though it requires a good deal more preparation time. In the One Minute Apology, there are no excuses, no self-victimization, no drama. It's simple, to the point, and very effective. *The time-consuming part comes in being completely honest with yourself and taking responsibility for your mistakes before you apologize.* Unless you do that—it will not be effective."

"I see," responded the young man thoughtfully.

"This may be your president's problem," said the One Minute Manager. "The failure of many leaders begins when they are unwilling to admit to themselves that they've done something wrong. It's their job to accept responsibility for their actions. In your president's case, he's captain of a ship that's going under fast. Unfortunately, in his situation, he isn't the only one going down with the ship—he's taking his crew with him.

"If you think about it, you'll discover that the core of most problems is the same," said the One Minute Manager. "Only the names, dates, and places change."

"What's at the core of most problems?" the young man asked.

✻

At The Core
Of
Most Problems
Is
A Truth
You Don't Want
To Face

✻

The One Minute Manager continued, "*Any problem you have spins out of control the minute you avoid dealing with the truth.*"

"I think you may have put your finger on my president's problem," the young man said. "When I first met him, I regarded him as a champion and model of integrity—someone who wanted to hear the truth. But as his success increased, he began to lose touch. His recent growing sense of self-importance has made it difficult for him to admit the truth and do the right thing. I'm even concerned that he may have lost sight of what the 'right thing' is."

"When people attempt to disassociate themselves from the truth, or pretend 'it never happened' or that 'it wasn't my fault'—they're in denial," observed the One Minute Manager. "Those in denial have lost touch with the truth. They can't apologize because they rationalize they're not at fault. They can never admit they are wrong."

"Why don't people want to face the truth?" wondered the young man.

"*Because they don't realize that it's the truth that will set them free,*" began the One Minute Manager. "*The truth is intolerant of deception.* There is either right or wrong. *The truth doesn't give people a lot of 'wiggle room' and for some, that can feel very uncomfortable—especially if you are living a lie.*"

The young man immediately caught on: "That helps explain why my president has become defensive and unwilling to listen to criticism. Lately if anyone tries to tell him the truth, he shoots the messenger. As a result, I've found myself keeping anyone or anything with negative information from my boss just to prevent him from getting angry and taking it out on me and the other members of the staff. The implications of what you are saying are getting to me. I'd like to think about what you've just told me."

"I think that's a good idea," said the One Minute Manager. "So why don't we call it a day?"

"I agree. So, have we covered the One Minute Apology?" the young man inquired.

"No, we've just been talking about the big picture. There are two vital parts of the One Minute Apology that we'll discuss tomorrow:

✿

A One Minute Apology
Begins With Surrender
And
Ends With Integrity

✿

"Annie will be arriving in the morning. Why don't you talk with her about the first part of the One Minute Apology—*Surrender.* She really knows the topic inside and out. Then, after breakfast, we're planning to motor across the lake to see someone who misses you, my mother, Nana. We're planning to help Nana pick vegetables from her garden for tomorrow night's dinner. That is, if you would like to join us. Nana has great advice about the second part of the One Minute Apology—*Integrity.* Later, in the afternoon, we can play golf, if you like."

"That sounds great about seeing Nana again and playing golf, but shouldn't I be concentrating on solving the problem at hand?" the young man wondered.

The One Minute Manager responded, "*A balanced life is not all work—it's having some fun too.* Being able to take time to do something you enjoy while you're solving problems is a sign that you are mastering your life."

"My father told me I could always trust you to steer me in the right direction," the young man said as he walked toward his room. "My dad was right! See you in the morning!"

"Good night," replied the One Minute Manager.

Surrender

Saturday morning, the young man awoke at 7:00 A.M., went to the kitchen, and made a pot of coffee. He took his journal and coffee outside, being careful not to disturb anyone. When he got to the end of the dock, he sat down and opened his journal to review his notes from the previous night.

Engrossed in his concerns about his problem at work, the young man was interrupted by the sound of tires on the gravel road above. He looked up to see the One Minute Manager, Carol, and Brad greet the driver of the car. He knew from their enthusiasm that it had to be Annie. The young man leapt up from his place on the dock and went up the stairs two at a time.

As he approached, Annie called to him, "Dad said you were going to be here. It's great to see you."

They hugged and the young man said, "My visit has already become more than I hoped. Here, let me take your bag."

"Who's hungry?" asked Carol.

"We're famished!" was the general consensus.

Over breakfast the young man brought the conversation back to the One Minute Apology. He said he really needed to find an answer to his pressing problem. The One Minute Manager turned to his daughter and asked, "Annie, would you feel comfortable talking about—*surrendering and admitting you were wrong?*"

"Considering all the practice I've had, I'd love to!" she replied.

Everyone laughed as they recalled some of Annie's outrageous teenage escapades.

When the kidding subsided, Annie began.

"The surrendering process of the One Minute Apology has two important parts. The first is about *you* and coming to grips with what *you* did wrong. The second is making sure the person or persons you have harmed feel that *you* know you made a mistake.

"To surrender, you first let go of being right, and then confront the truth about your own failings by being one hundred percent honest with yourself. A fundamental concept to remember is:

＊

One Minute
Of Being Honest
With Yourself
Is Worth More Than
Days, Months, Or Years
Of
Self-Deception

＊

"Kidding yourself is an expensive habit that has no reward," said Annie, smiling.

"So, self-deception comes at a high price," the young man agreed.

"Once you are honest with yourself," said Annie, "then you must take full responsibility for your actions and the harm you've done to someone else. That requires both humility and courage. Dad often says that great leaders give everyone else credit when things go well. And when things go wrong, they take full responsibility. However, self-centered leaders take the credit when things go well and blame everyone else when things go wrong."

The latter describes my president's behavior in front of the board yesterday, thought the young man.

"When you surrender, you let go of the story you have told yourself, and realize you need to apologize to those you have offended, regardless of the outcome," Annie said.

"How do you make sure anyone you have harmed feels that you know you made a mistake?" asked the young man.

"First, *you feel it yourself. Then you take action as soon as possible.* Remember:

✿

The Longer You Wait
To Apologize,
The Sooner
Your Weakness Is
Perceived As Wickedness

✿

"We all make mistakes and fall short of perfection. *What can make us seem evil in the eyes of others is their belief that if we can't be truthful about this incident, we probably lie about other things too.*"

"If that's the case, why don't people apologize sooner?" asked the young man.

The One Minute Manager added: "To some people, apologizing is regarded as a weakness rather than a strength. Maybe that's why that saying, 'Love means never having to say you're sorry' became so popular in the 70's. A lot of people thought it was a wonderful saying. And yet, what a selfish statement that is. I'd like to rephrase that sentence to read, 'Love is being able to say I'm sorry and mean it.' "

"Why is apologizing seen as a weakness?" wondered the young man aloud.

"It all comes down to a need many people have of always trying to look good and be right," replied Annie.

"The problem with trying to be right all the time is that usually someone else has to be wrong," said Brad.

"Exactly," said Annie. "What an exhausting way to live—trying to be right all the time. If people would give up the need to 'be right' and apologies were accepted as a legitimate response to making mistakes, then honesty and sincerity would replace 'cover-ups'!"

Annie continued, "And things could be made right for those who have been hurt or harmed."

"I see," said the young man. "Apologizing isn't just about you or me, it's also about the person wronged."

"Right. The next step makes that even clearer. You have to *be specific*," said Annie, *"and tell the people harmed exactly what you're apologizing for."*

Brad laughed. "When Annie and I were young, we were experts at not being specific about what we did wrong. If Mom or Dad caught us misbehaving, we'd say 'I'm sorry, I'm sorry, I'm sorry' until we were blue in the face."

"Did it work?" the young man asked with a twinkle in his eye.

"They *thought* it did," chuckled Carol.

When the laughter calmed Annie continued, "After you tell someone specifically what you did wrong, the last step is *sharing how you feel about what you did*—embarrassed, sad, ashamed. *And that you feel bad enough to change your behavior.* By doing so you make your apology real and demonstrate your sincerity."

"Without sharing your feelings and a change in behavior," said the One Minute Manager, "an apology will seem mechanical—as if you are going through the motions without being personally involved."

"Maybe it's a 'guy thing,' but I find describing my feelings one of the hardest things for me to do, especially in a situation where I am feeling badly or embarrassed about what I have done," admitted the young man.

"It's not easy for anyone to admit they are wrong. That's what I meant a few minutes ago when I said it takes both courage *and* humility."

"Changing my behavior also sounds easier than it probably is," said the young man.

"Yes, and that takes desire. When you have the desire, self-discipline becomes easy," said the One Minute Manager.

"I see what you mean," said the young man. "I want to make sure I'm getting this surrender process right. Let me summarize what I've learned so far." Referring to his notes, he led them through his understanding of how surrendering makes a One Minute Apology work:

A One Minute Apology
Begins With Surrender

You Surrender When You:

- *Are truthful and admit to yourself that you've done something wrong and need to make up for it.*

- *Take full responsibility for your actions and any harm done to anyone else.*

- *Have a sense of urgency about apologizing—you act as soon as possible.*

- *Tell everyone you've harmed exactly what you now realize was your mistake—you are very specific.*

- *Share with those you harmed how badly you feel about what you did— enough to change your behavior and not do it again.*

Integrity

Y ou're a quick learner," said the One Minute Manager. "Your reward is a special game of golf this afternoon!"

After breakfast, Carol said she wanted to finish reading her book. Everyone else headed to the boat to ride across the lake to visit with Nana and pick some of her vegetables.

After docking they walked up a stone path to the house. A woman in a wide-brimmed gardening hat, overalls, and flowered canvas gloves, came out from behind the stalks of corn. It was Nana.

On her right was a flourishing vegetable garden filled with corn, zucchini, string beans, carrots, cucumbers, a variety of lettuces, and eggplant. "I'm getting some great vegetables this year. Are you here to gather some for dinner?"

"Absolutely!" said the One Minute Manager. "In fact, we brought along an extra pair of hands. You remember Bill and Betty's son?"

"I'm so happy to see you back with us. We've missed you," Nana said with a warm smile.

"Thank you, Nana," replied the young man. "What an amazing garden. I've never seen such huge vegetables! You certainly have a green thumb!"

"All I do is plant the seeds. Nature is very forgiving of any mistakes I might make," Nana added.

"We have been talking about making mistakes," he said, "and the need for apologizing for them."

"So, you are learning the One Minute Apology?"

"Indeed I am," said the young man. "I've learned about surrender, now I need to find out about the *integrity* part of the One Minute Apology. Your son tells me that you have a lot of wisdom on the subject."

Nana smiled and said, "That's kind. My husband—Annie and Brad's grandfather—used to tell us, 'When all is said and done, the most important thing we have is our integrity.' "

"I certainly agree, but I have a question. Is there a difference between honesty and integrity?" asked the young man.

"Yes," said Nana and added:

✴

Honesty
Is Telling The Truth
To Ourselves And Others

Integrity
Is Living That Truth

✴

"So when you surrender, you demonstrate your honesty," the young man reasoned, "and integrity is all about 'walking your talk.' "

"Good point," said Nana. "Integrity means consistency. It is being the kind of person you want to be regardless of the situation. That involves making wrongs right."

"How do you determine the kind of person you want to be?" asked the young man.

"You might try writing your own obituary," said the One Minute Manager with a smile. "As a matter of fact I've written my own."

"Excuse me, but that sounds kind of morbid," said the young man. "Why would you want to do that?"

The One Minute Manager chuckled, saying, "I became interested in writing my own obituary after I heard a story about Alfred Nobel."

"Of Nobel Peace Prize fame?"

"Yes," said the One Minute Manager. "It's interesting, even though the Nobel Prize is also given for Science, Economics, Literature, Medicine, and Chemistry, Nobel is best known for the Peace Prize. And yet he wasn't always associated with peace. You might recall from history that Alfred Nobel was also involved with the invention of dynamite."

"Now that you mention it, I do," said the young man.

"Well," continued the One Minute Manager, "When Nobel's brother died, Alfred got a copy of the local Stockholm newspaper and discovered that they had somehow mixed up the two brothers.

"As a result, Alfred Nobel had the very unique experience of reading his own obituary with his morning coffee. Can you imagine what that must have felt like?"

"Was the central message of his obituary about his involvement with dynamite?" asked the young man.

"It was," said the One Minute Manager. "Nobel was devastated to think that he would be remembered only for destruction. As a result, he redesigned his life so he would be especially remembered for honoring the pursuit of world peace. It became his driving force. How you want others to think about you now and in the future can influence your desire to apologize."

"So," said the young man, "are you suggesting that besides attempting to right a wrong, a One Minute Apology is a way to realign your behavior with your self-image?"

"That's a good way to think about it," said the One Minute Manager. "One of my favorite sayings is:

�֍

The Legacy
You Leave
Is
The One
You Live

�֍

"We all fall short of perfection," said Nana. "As a result, we all sometimes do things that are inconsistent with the legacy we want to leave. Your integrity is measured by how quickly you correct your mistakes and get back on course."

"When you treat other people better by correcting the mistakes you made with them, you must feel pretty good about yourself," said the young man.

"Absolutely," said Nana. "You have to continually reaffirm your own worth and good intentions. You're fine, it's your behavior that trips you up once in a while. *Never get upset with yourself—only with your behavior.*"

"You're hitting home with me. When my behavior is inconsistent with who I want to be, I have a difficult time getting a good night's rest until I correct my mistake," observed the young man.

"Like Abraham Lincoln," added Nana.

"Abraham Lincoln?" responded the young man.

"He's one of my heroes," smiled Nana. "Carl Sandburg in one of his books wrote about a lapse in Abraham Lincoln's behavior that I reread from time to time to help me remember that *everyone* makes mistakes. Why don't you and I take a break from the gardening so I can share that story with you."

Nana started toward her cottage, motioning for the young man to follow. When they got to the porch, Nana told the young man to have a seat while she found the book.

When she returned, Nana opened the book to the bookmarked page and handed it to the young man. "This story shows how the challenges of leadership can test who you truly want to be."

The young man began to read:

During the Civil War President Abraham Lincoln was visited by Colonel Scott, one of the commanders of the troops guarding the Capitol from attack by the Confederate forces in Northern Virginia.

Scott's wife had drowned in a steamship collision in the Chesapeake Bay when returning home after a journey to Washington to nurse her sick husband.

Scott had appealed to regimental command for leave to attend her burial and comfort his children. His request had been denied; a battle seemed imminent and every officer was essential.

But Scott, as was his right, had pressed his request up the chain of command until it reached the Secretary of War, Edwin Stanton. Since Stanton had also denied the request, the colonel had taken his appeal all the way to the top.

Scott got to his Commander in Chief in the presidential office late on a Saturday night, the last visitor allowed in. Lincoln listened to the story and as Scott recalled his response, the President exploded, "Am I to have no rest? Is there no hour or spot when or where I may escape these constant requests? Why do you follow me here with such business as this? Why do you not go to the War Office where they have charge of all matters of papers and transportation?"

Scott told Lincoln of Stanton's refusal, and the President replied, "Then you probably ought not to go down the river. Mr. Stanton knows all about the necessities of the hour; he knows what rules are necessary, and the rules are made to be enforced.

"It would be wrong of me to override his rules and decisions of this kind: it might work disaster to important movements. And then, you ought to remember that I have other duties to attend to—heaven knows, enough for one man—and I can give no thought to questions of this kind. Why do you come here to appeal to my humanity?

"Don't you know we are in the midst of a war? That suffering and death press upon all of us? That works of humanity and affection, which we cheerfully perform in days of peace, are all trampled upon and outlawed by war? That there is no room left for them? There is but one duty now—to fight!

"Every family in the land is crushed with sorrow; but they must not each come to me for help. I have all the burdens I can carry. Go to the War Department. Your business belongs there.

"If they cannot help you, then bear your burden, as we all must, until this war is over. Everything must yield to the paramount duty of finishing this war." Colonel Scott returned to his barrack, brooding.

When the young man finished reading the passage, he looked up and asked, "Is that a true story?"

Nana nodded, "Yes."

"It just doesn't sound like the Lincoln I read about in school," continued the young man. "I'm surprised by his behavior. When I say I'm surprised, I'm not talking about his decision to deny Scott leave. Given the circumstances, that may have been the right decision. But I always pictured Lincoln as selfless, caring, and compassionate, so I am a little shocked by the way he treated Scott."

"So your image of Lincoln was shaken a little," commented Nana.

"That's a good way to put it," said the young man. "He showed no compassion about Scott's wife's sudden death."

The young man began to read again:

Am I to have no rest? Why do you follow me here with such business as this? . . . You ought to remember that I have other duties to attend to—heaven knows, enough for one man . . . I have all the burdens I can carry.

"What do you think was happening that might have caused Lincoln to behave like that?" asked Nana.

"Well, the burden of the war was weighing on him, with all the suffering and the death. It was also the end of the day, and he had to be exhausted. So, I can see why Lincoln might have behaved as he did," said the young man.

"Maybe," said Nana. "But there is a big difference between an explanation of why something happened and an excuse. An explanation deals with the reasons why something happened, while an excuse tries to cover up who's to blame and establish a reason to minimize accountability. *You can always find an excuse for your poor behavior if you lie to yourself.*"

"You have a point," admitted the young man. "But that still doesn't sound like Lincoln."

"Do you think Lincoln would have liked this story to be a part of his obituary?"

"I doubt it," smiled the young man. "I don't think it would fit the image he had of himself."

"Why don't you turn the page and read the next paragraphs," suggested Nana. So the young man did.

Early the next morning, Colonel Scott heard a rap at the door. He opened it and there stood the President. He took Scott's hands, held them and broke out: *"My dear Colonel, I was a brute last night. I have no excuse to offer.*

"I was weary to the last extent, but I had no right to treat a man with rudeness who has offered his life to his country, much more a man in great affliction. I have had a regretful night and now come to beg your forgiveness."

He said he had arranged with Stanton for Scott to go to his wife's funeral. In his own carriage the Commander-In-Chief took the colonel to the steamer wharf of the Potomac and wished him Godspeed.

"What a wonderful One Minute Apology," said the young man. "It was not just his words. Lincoln's behavior made the apology powerful."

"I thought you would enjoy that," agreed Nana.

"Lincoln was willing to surrender and admit to himself that he'd done something wrong," said the young man. "He took full responsibility for his actions, and sincerely recognized the need to apologize to the person he had offended."

"He also acted as soon as possible—*early the next morning,*" reviewed Nana. "He was specific—*'I was a brute last night. . . . I had no right to treat a man with rudeness who has offered his life to his country, much more a man in great affliction . . . ,'* and he showed how he felt about what he did—*'I have had a regretful night.'*"

"Sounds like you memorized that passage," added the young man.

"I told you I was a Lincoln fan," smiled Nana. "In addition to being a great example of what my son means by surrendering in a One Minute Apology, Lincoln also demonstrated his integrity."

"How?"

"He didn't send for Scott, he went to Scott's quarters himself. The night before he kept insisting that Scott follows the chain of command, but in the light of the day, Lincoln couldn't have cared less about the hierarchy. In many ways, he was saying, 'The way I treated you last night was wrong—I am not proud of that man at all. The man you met last night just isn't me at all.'"

"To admit those things would be tough for many people," said the young man.

"That's true," Nana agreed, adding, "Sometimes when we're wrong it affects our self-image or pride too much to admit it and then forgive ourselves. The wrong seems like such a violation, we can't get past it."

"Forgive *ourselves*? What do you mean?"

"When people realize the terrible harm they've done, often they are unable to forgive themselves. They feel dreadful about what they've done to hurt or disappoint someone else," said Nana.

"The concept of forgiving yourself sounds simple. But it's not always easy to do," she added.

"What makes it so difficult?" asked the young man.

Nana responded, "You have to deal with two facts: first you did something wrong to someone else that needs to be corrected. Second, you did something that is at odds with who you want to be, or how you want others to think of you. You ask yourself questions like, *What did I do?* and *Why did I do it? Was it a random, impulsive, thoughtless act? Was it in anger? Was it calculated? Is it becoming a pattern in my behavior? Am I better than my inconsiderate behavior?*"

"I imagine Lincoln asked himself those kinds of questions during his regretful night," said the young man.

"Undoubtedly," said Nana. "He must have reminded himself who he really was and then resolved to become that person again. Thus his early morning visit to Scott's quarters."

"Do you think Lincoln's reversal of his decision not to allow Scott to attend his wife's funeral was done because of guilt?" wondered the young man.

"No, I think Lincoln realized he was wrong," said Nana. "Lincoln knew how much he had hurt Scott and decided that he should make amends personally."

"Making amends shows you are genuinely sincere about earning back lost trust," said the young man.

"But you make amends only when you change your behavior and make up for what you did," said Nana. *"And in a way the other person can appreciate."*

The young man said, "Like the way Lincoln took Scott to the train in his own carriage?"

"Yes," said Nana. "Aren't you more likely to do business with a person who tries to recover your goodwill by making amends?"

"Yes," answered the young man. "Recently an airline lost my reservation. I was very upset and said so to the ticket agent. After she admitted that it was a systems error and apologized for the inconvenience they had caused me, she said, 'This is so unlike us. I just put a note into the computer to make sure this doesn't happen again, but I do want to see if I can do anything right now to regain your loyalty.'

"I was impressed and told her, 'You already have because you listened to me, admitted the airline had erred, and asked how you could make up for it right now.'"

"Asking how she could make up for any harm done," continued Nana, "showed how sincere she was about earning back lost trust. Most people appreciate a sincere apology and are as eager to put the incident behind them as you were. But *a One Minute Apology is incomplete without a sincere attempt to make things right.*"

✷

Without A Change In
Your Behavior,
Just Saying
"I'm Sorry"
Is Not Enough

✷

"Then what is enough?" asked the young man.

Nana responded, "The only way you can demonstrate that you are really sorry is by changing your behavior. That way the person you have harmed knows that you are committed to not repeating what you did."

"Is that why people dismiss it when someone just says 'I'm sorry'?" asked the young man.

"Yes, if you're unreliable time and time again, and you say 'I'm sorry,' no one will take you seriously," replied Nana.

The young man nodded, catching the full implication.

"Right! Now let's go see how our gardeners are doing," said Nana as she got up from her porch chair and headed back down the path. The young man jotted down a few notes and followed her.

When they arrived at the garden, the One Minute Manager, who by now had a basket filled with string beans and carrots, asked, "Well, can you now appreciate the value of integrity in a One Minute Apology?"

"I sure can," answered the young man. "Let me review my notes with you:

The One Minute Apology
Ends With Integrity

You Have Integrity When You:

- *Recognize that what you did or failed to do is wrong and is inconsistent with who you want to be.*

- *Reaffirm that you are better than your poor behavior and forgive yourself.*

- *Recognize how much you have hurt others, and make amends to them for the harm you caused.*

- *Make a commitment to yourself and others not to repeat the act, and demonstrate your commitment by changing your behavior.*

"Good work," said the One Minute Manager.

Turning to Nana, the young man said, "Thank you for teaching me about integrity. I particularly enjoyed that wonderful Lincoln story—there's someone I'd like to share it with."

"It's nice to know it means that much to you," said Nana. Then she smiled. "You all better head back to the house. Carol wants these vegetables for dinner tonight."

Everyone gave Nana a good-bye hug, loaded the vegetables in the boat, and began the trip back across the lake.

"See you for dinner, Nana," said Brad as they pulled away from the dock.

"Thank you all for the help," Nana said as they waved good-bye.

Not Attached To Outcome

After they unloaded and rinsed Nana's vegetables the young man and the One Minute Manager left for the golf course. They had a quick sandwich and as they approached the first tee, the One Minute Manager turned to the young man and said, "Since you haven't played golf in a while, why don't we play N.A.T.O. golf today instead of competitive golf?"

"N.A.T.O. golf?"

"Yes. N.A.T.O. stands for Not Attached To Outcome. When most people play golf, they focus only on their results and how they look to others. Their score becomes who they are. I'd like you to see how well you hit the ball when you're focusing on 'the game' instead of the 'results.' "

"That sounds like fun," said the young man. "But knowing you, this won't be just a golf lesson."

"True," said the One Minute Manager, smiling. "N.A.T.O. applies to the One Minute Apology too. *Your apology should not be attached to the outcome or response you get—whether the people forgive you or not.* Remember:

✵

Apologize
Not For The Outcome
But
Because You Know
You Were Wrong
And It's
The Right Thing
To Do

✵

By the time they finished playing golf and returned to the house, dinner was being prepared. Carol gave the young man a bag of corn to shuck and asked, "So who won?"

"We both did," replied the young man.

"Oh, you played N.A.T.O. golf?"

"We sure did! It's amazing what you can do when you don't worry about your performance, the outcome, or the opinion of others. It was the most fun I've had playing golf in a long time. The N.A.T.O. approach can be applied to just about anything."

"Yes, it can," said Carol with a knowing smile. "My husband has a very unique way of teaching his insights. Have you thought of ways you might apply it?"

"Yes. N.A.T.O is already helping me to be more engaged in what I'm doing here, instead of worrying about what might happen next week at work."

"I have every confidence that you will have everything you need to know by the time you leave," said Carol.

Apology At Home And At Work

Just as the dinner preparation was completed, Nana arrived. She walked in carrying a large envelope and handed it to the young man, saying, "You said how much you enjoyed the story of Lincoln. I had it copied for you."

"How incredibly thoughtful of you!" he said as he opened the envelope. "You can't imagine what this means to me." Then turning to the One Minute Manager, he said, "I would love to share this with someone. Would you mind if I used your fax machine? I'd like to send it to my president."

"Go right ahead," said the One Minute Manager.

As the young man returned to join the others, the doorbell rang. Carol opened the door and introduced everyone to their new neighbors, Gayle and Don.

Conversation started with stories of how they all happened to be at the lake that weekend. When it was the young man's turn, he said he came for the One Minute Manager's advice about a problem at work, but had ended up learning a powerful new secret that he knew would change the course of his life. The neighbors were immediately curious.

The young man shared with Gayle and Don all that he had learned about the One Minute Apology.

"The subject of apology is very interesting," said Don thoughtfully. "I would bet most people, including myself, don't really know how to apologize effectively so they just avoid it. And yet when people don't have the guts to admit they were wrong, a small matter can get totally out of control. In some cases, becomes even newsworthy."

"People don't seem to know how or when to apologize," Carol remarked, "and they find themselves mumbling 'excuse me' or 'I'm sorry.' It's a feeble gesture that has absolutely no impact on the other person."

"That happened to me once at school," said Brad. "I tried to apologize to my biology teacher. I can still remember the look in her eyes—as if to say, 'I don't believe a word you are saying!' "

"How did you handle that?" asked Annie.

"I had to convince her I was sincere. I went to her classroom after school and said how badly I felt about letting the hamsters loose. I then offered to replace them and stay to help her correct papers. Her expression showed she still questioned my sincerity and said she didn't need my help.

"I looked out the window at the parking lot and saw her car. It was filthy. I asked her if I could clean her car. She looked surprised. I could see she was not about to trust me with it.

"I took the time to persuade her to let me do something special for her. I think I finally regained her respect when I followed through and washed her car once a month for the rest of the semester."

"How did you know she respected you?" asked Annie.

"I could see it in her eyes and in the thoughtful way she began to talk to me."

"That's a good example, Brad," said Don. "Maybe you can offer me some advice. I just found out that an old friend of mine is angry with me because he thinks I did something unethical to him. He never mentioned anything to me. Now I know why he cut off contact with me. What should I do? Even though I don't feel I did anything wrong, should I apologize to him?"

"Not if you didn't do anything wrong, intentionally or unintentionally," answered Brad. "I don't think an apology would be appropriate in that case."

"You're right, Brad. *Never apologize just to appease someone,*" added the One Minute Manager. "Then you are only being dishonest with yourself. Have you looked honestly at whether you *did* do something wrong that you don't want to see?

"When there are conflicting views about the need for an apology, conflict resolution is the real issue. If you want to repair the relationship, you need to have a neutral mediator listen to each side and help them come to a workable solution," continued the One Minute Manager.

Gayle joined the conversation and said, "I'm the human resources director at my company. The One Minute Apology could be useful for problems where I work. What would you do if a person you work with swears you did something wrong to them, but you don't remember it?"

The One Minute Manager answered, "First *listen* to the other person. Ask questions and be ready to realize you *did* make a mistake, even if you were not aware of it. Then, you can tell the person *your* truth— you wouldn't intentionally cause them harm, and yet it pains you to see them troubled."

Then he added, "*Just because you don't remember the incident doesn't mean you didn't cause any harm.*

"You may have considered the incident as trivial or were too busy or thoughtless to think about how your actions affected that person. Discounting someone's words, his or her opinions and ideas can be damaging to that person. It feels like you are dismissing *them*. If you have a pattern of harmful behavior, you may be at fault."

"Assure them you didn't mean to hurt them and want to correct the situation," suggested Annie.

"What if you don't particularly like the person to whom you need to apologize?" asked Gayle.

"It may seem difficult at first, but whether or not you like them shouldn't matter," replied the One Minute Manager. *"You apologize because it is the right thing to do."*

"I could use some help overcoming negative feelings about someone. I find the person draining," said Gayle.

"If you don't like someone, then you might ask yourself, 'What is preventing me from liking that person?' " suggested Annie.

"Mother, why don't you tell us about your recent river trip in British Columbia," suggested the One Minute Manager.

"It's interesting you mention that," said Nana. "I was just thinking about it myself. There were twenty-five of us on that river trip. It was June but freezing cold. There had been a lot of snow in Canada that winter, so the river was higher than normal.

"Our guides discussed the unusual conditions but none of us were worried enough to turn back. There were two families with children, and the rest were couples. One man was facially scarred and disfigured and, frankly, looked very mean. Behind his back the children called him 'Scarface' and were frightened not only by his looks, but also by the way he spoke. He had a gruff voice that made every word sound like a snarl. He and his wife stayed to themselves and weren't the least bit sociable. That suited most everyone else just fine.

"Midway through the trip, we traveled by van on a narrow dirt road for two hours to get to another leg of the river. On the way, the truck with all our provisions broke down right in front of the van. Our van couldn't get past the truck.

"We were hundreds of miles away from the nearest town and no one expected us to show up for another nine days. Our cell phones were out of range. We were stuck in the woods!

"It became colder and began to snow. Everyone bundled together to keep warm, except the scarred man and his wife. They went for a walk instead!

"The boatmen tried time and again to get the truck started. No luck. We were all becoming a little frightened.

"After a while, the scarred man returned and asked, in his gruff manner, what the holdup was. The boatmen said they didn't know why the truck wouldn't start. The frightening-looking man tried the engine. Nothing happened.

"He opened the hood and began to tinker. Next, he started to take apart the engine. Now everyone was on the edge of panic—the kids were yelling that 'Scarface' was wrecking the engine. But we were too afraid to confront him.

"Finally, I figured I was too old to put up with anybody's craziness so I went up to ask what the heck he was doing. He turned to me and growled, 'See if anyone has tweezers, a piece of wire, or a bobby pin!' His tone was harsh but his eyes were bright and full of confidence.

"I helped find the things he was looking for," Nana said. "An hour later, he had the truck repaired. Everyone—and I do mean everyone—especially the kids, started applauding and hooting and hollering! 'You saved our lives!' they yelled. He just blushed, smiled for the first time, and said, 'It wasn't much. Anyone could have done it.'

"Of course we all knew otherwise. From that moment on, his new nickname was 'Hero,' " Nana said, relating the story with pleasure.

"The kids began to idolize him, and every night they listened while he told stories of the wild adventures he had in his past. He'd had plenty, mind you! As it turned out, he was a fireman. His face had been severely burned saving eight kindergartners trapped in a fire.

"We gathered around the campfire on our last night. I'll never forget the words from the brattiest kid of the trip. He stood up and said he could never forgive himself if he didn't apologize in front of everyone for the terrible way he had treated Hero.

"He said Hero didn't just save his life, he saved him from treating anyone like that ever again. Hero stood up, took the kid in his arms, lifted him in the air, and hugged him.

"Hero looked him in the eyes and said, 'When I was your age, I was much worse! And I owe you an apology too—I was anything but friendly when I joined the group.

"'I assumed you all were like a lot of other people I've been around lately. I judged you too. I didn't have the confidence to allow you to know the "real me." I apologize and I assure you I won't make that mistake again,' he said.

"By the final day of the trip, no one wanted to say good-bye. No one wanted the trip to end," said Nana.

The young man responded, "I can see why. They believed Hero because they saw him change from an antisocial person to an active participant. He got involved and transformed the entire group with his actions. Who would want to leave such an experience?"

"When we sincerely apologize, forgive ourselves, make amends, and demonstrate we've changed, we have more peace of mind. Those around us can then have peace of mind too," said Nana. *"Peace of mind—* isn't it strange how something that doesn't cost anything and is within our grasp at all times can often feel so far away?"

The group became pensive. Carol and Annie directed everyone to the buffet dinner, and they all quietly helped themselves. The young man thought to himself, "Peace of mind—that's certainly something my president doesn't have right now. And come to think of it, neither do I."

Gayle was the first to speak. "What if you remember something you meant to do, and now you feel it's much too late to do anything about it?"

"Can you give us an example?" asked Carol.

"Yes. About ten years ago, the husband of a friend I worked with died. I was on a business trip and promised myself to send her flowers and a personal letter. I never did either and all these years I have felt badly. If I saw this person today on the sidewalk, I'd be tempted to cross to the other side of the street from sheer embarrassment."

Carol answered, "Just pick up the phone and call her. *Never assume you know what another person is thinking*. It may make her feel very special that you called her to apologize after all these years—you have an opportunity to strengthen or restore a relationship."

"That's just what I'll do," Gayle replied. "I'm beginning to think of more possibilities for the One Minute Apology, especially at work.

"Yesterday a young sales manager came to me for advice. He said he had given his boss a marketing idea that his assistant had thought of, and yet he hadn't credited her. He was concerned the promotion he's getting is partially because of her idea. He wasn't sure how to handle it with either his boss or his assistant."

"What happened next?" asked Carol.

"He went back to his boss, and explained what happened. His boss said the recent marketing idea was not the reason that he been promoted. But now there was another, even better reason—he was a manager with integrity!

"He was relieved, but said he still wants to clear up the matter with his assistant. He will feel much better when I go to work and tell him about an effective One Minute Apology," Gayle observed.

At the mention of returning to work the young man felt a sudden wave of anxiety. He reminded himself—*don't be attached to outcome* and returned to the discussion.

"At our company," said Don, "many office problems are a result of conflict, obnoxious behavior, pettiness, while others are a result of accidents, mistakes, assumptions, forgetfulness, or just plain stupidity."

"In those cases is there ever a good reason not to apologize?" the young man asked.

Annie asked, "If you made a stupid mistake, would you want to repeat it?"

"No," answered the young man.

"Would you feel badly if your mistake caused harm to others?" asked Annie.

"Yes, of course," the young man replied.

"Fine," smiled Annie. "So what's the answer?"

"Anytime I make a mistake, or harm or dismiss someone by accident or purposefully, a One Minute Apology is in order right away," he said.

"It seems to me," said the young man:

✻

The Best Way To Apologize
To Someone You Have Harmed
Is To Tell Them
You Made A Mistake,
You Feel Badly About It,
And
How You
Will Change Your Behavior

✻

"That's an easy way to remember it," said Don.

The young man added, "And every apology I make will help me be more aware of the impact my behavior has on others and will teach me to be more sensitive and considerate in the future. Then I can affect others and ultimately make them more sensitive about the effects of their behavior and help them eliminate *their* need to apologize. *It's all about Apology Prevention—isn't it?*"

"You *got* it. You *really* got it!" exclaimed the One Minute Manager, beaming at the young man.

Don noticed how late it was. "I can't believe we stayed so long! We have had a wonderful time this evening. What a great conversation. No chitchat in this house. Thank you all very much."

Gayle walked to the front door speaking to the One Minute Manager, "If it's all right with you, I'd like to call you next week. I want to include the One Minute Apology in our human resources manual. We could put it to good use in our company right away."

"I'll look forward to that," answered the One Minute Manager.

The young man excused himself and wrote down:

✿

*Every One Minute Apology
Makes You More Aware
Of
How Much Your Behavior
Affects Others*

✿

Taking Responsibility

Sunday morning the young man woke up to the sound of thunder. It was dark, gray, and windy, with lightning in the distance. He looked at the alarm clock and saw that it was only 6:30 A.M. But he felt rested and jumped out of bed to get ready for his final day at the lake. He went into the kitchen and as he was making a pot of coffee, he heard a voice behind him.

"There's nothing like the smell of coffee in the morning!" It was Annie. "What are you doing up so early?"

"I was about to ask you the same thing," he responded.

"Would you like to enjoy your coffee outside on the covered porch?" she asked.

"Yes. I enjoy the rain," answered the young man as he opened the door to the deck.

"Is the weekend turning out the way you had hoped?" Annie asked.

"On my flight here I thought—this is great! I'll be seeing your father and with his advice, all my problems will be solved. The reality is that everyone I've been with this weekend has given me a new perspective."

"My mother says that when you are willing to be a student, the necessary teachers appear."

"I've learned so much this weekend: I now see that *if you lie to yourself, lying to others becomes second nature.* I've learned that as difficult as it may be, the first thing to do when I've done something wrong is come to grips with the fact that I made a mistake. The more typical thing is to try to make excuses for what I did wrong, or justify it somehow. I will now take what I do seriously and admit my mistakes, have a sense of urgency about apologizing to those I have hurt, and let them know exactly how I feel. I make amends in a way that lets the other person know I am sincere—but most of all I realize that *trust doesn't return until the person I've offended is convinced I have changed my behavior.*"

"You have learned a lot," Annie said. "I know what you mean. These family discussions are important to me. That's why I enjoy coming home whenever I can. One lesson I've learned over and over from my parents is *culpability.*"

"What do you mean by that?" he asked.

"Well, it's not a lesson anyone enjoys hearing.

"Culpability is our part in the problem—or what we did to contribute to the situation. Sometimes it's because of an action we've taken, but more often than not, it's the result of inaction, because we haven't been honest with ourselves or others."

"Sometimes it's difficult to tell the truth. No one enjoys reporting bad news and most people don't take bad news well," he commented. The young man paused as a startling thought occurred to him, "Aha! Annie, are you trying to tell me in a very nice, polite way that I may have contributed in some way to my boss's problem? Like, maybe I didn't do something I should have done? Am I culpable?"

"That's not for me to say. I really don't know what happened. You know Dad would never break a confidence," replied Annie.

"Still, what you say strikes a chord. I really have to think about my own culpability. I won't run away from the idea. But blaming others is *soooo* much easier," he said with a grin.

Annie laughed. Then she said, "Only in the short run. In the long run—well, I don't need to tell you the rest," she laughed.

"Thank you for the wake-up call," he replied.

"You're welcome. But it's nothing you wouldn't have figured out for yourself in time."

"Yes, but I have to turn into a genius by tomorrow morning," he protested.

A bright flash of lightning and an ear-splitting crack of thunder interrupted their talk.

"It doesn't look like you and Dad are going to play much golf today with all this lightning."

"Knowing the way your father thinks, he'll say 'Great day for golf—we'll have the course to ourselves!' "

"Do you really think you have him figured out?" asked Annie, laughing.

At that moment the One Minute Manager joined them. "Well, it looks like we'll have the golf course to ourselves!" he boomed.

"What did I tell you?" laughed the young man.

"I take back what I said. Maybe you will become a genius by tomorrow!" quipped Annie.

"What's all this laughing about?" Carol called as she walked to the porch from the kitchen. "Certainly not the weather!"

The smell of breakfast welcomed them as they made their way inside.

Self-Appreciation

At breakfast the young man said how much he enjoyed the dinner party and the discussion with the neighbors. He said, "I still have a few questions. What stops people from being honest and admitting they are wrong and then apologizing?"

"It's an inside job," answered the One Minute Manager.

"An inside job?" wondered the young man.

"It has to do with how you feel about yourself inside—your *self-appreciation*," said the One Minute Manager.

"How does a person learn to appreciate themself?" asked the young man.

"From four sources," replied the One Minute Manager. "The first is *fate*. At birth, you don't have a choice of where you are born, who your parents are, or whether you are male or female, or the color of your skin. It is fate.

"The second is your *early life experiences with adults*—your parents, relatives, teachers, and coaches.

"Third," continued the One Minute Manager, "are your *successes and failures in life*.

"And the fourth source of self-worth is *your perception of the first three*. Which of these four do you think is the most powerful?" asked the One Minute Manager.

"The fourth," the young man replied.

"Absolutely," said the One Minute Manager, "and from that perception you make all of your choices."

"Choices?" asked the young man.

"Yes," replied the One Minute Manager. "Regardless of our fate or our early experiences with adults, or our successes and failures in life—*we choose whether or not we appreciate ourselves*."

"Why would anyone *choose* to be negative about themselves?" asked the young man.

"That's where belief in your own value, apart from your past experiences, comes in, and that requires a different focus," said Carol.

"Our grandfather used to tell us," Brad began, "when a person loses perspective and comes to see themself as the center of the universe—that's the sign of an out-of-control ego."

"How does ego get out of control?" asked the young man.

"In two ways," insisted the One Minute Manager. "The first way is with *false pride*. That's when you think more of yourself than you should—when you're constantly promoting yourself ahead of others. When good things occur, you want all the credit."

"People like that are not very much fun to work with," smiled the young man. "They're always blowing their own horn."

"That's for sure," said the One Minute Manager. "The second way your ego gets you in trouble is *self-doubt*. That's when you think less of yourself than you should. Your emphasis then is on protecting yourself."

"I imagine that you would contend that people with false pride and self-doubt both have trouble apologizing," said the young man.

"Absolutely," interjected Annie. "People with false pride don't like to share their vulnerabilities. Admitting that they were wrong about something is their worst nightmare."

Brad jumped in: "And people with self-doubt are afraid to admit they are wrong because they fear that others will find out how incompetent they are."

"In both cases," continued the One Minute Manager, "their self-appreciation is external—they think who they are is a function of their performance, plus the opinions of others. As a result, their self-worth varies from day to day, depending on how people react to them. They think the world revolves around them. They lack humility. They don't realize that:

People With Humility
Don't Think Less
Of Themselves.
They Just Think
About Themselves Less

"How can you develop that kind of perspective?" asked the young man.

"You have to intentionally separate who you are from what you do," answered the One Minute Manager.

"You mean N.A.T.O.?" asked the young man.

"Absolutely," said the One Minute Manager smiling, "Not Attached To Outcome."

He continued, "When I ask parents, 'Do you love your kids?' they laugh because the answer is so obvious—of course they do. Then I ask, 'Do you love your kids only when they are successful? If they are successful, you'll love them, if they aren't successful you won't?' They laugh again and say, 'No. We love our kids no matter what.' That's unconditional love. What do you think would happen if you accepted that kind of unconditional love for yourself?"

"I'd be more secure and feel more positive about myself," answered the young man.

"That's for sure," said the One Minute Manager.

"The sad thing is that when you think the love you get is conditional, your self-worth is always up for grabs. That's when you start promoting or protecting yourself all the time. You believe you have to perform well or impress others to get any love or attention, and you have to repeat it again and again to keep it."

"That sounds like a shaky emotional foundation," the young man said as he helped the others clear the table.

"At some point," Carol said, leaning onto the table and looking directly at the young man, "you wake up and finally understand you can't achieve enough, gain enough recognition, obtain enough power, or own enough things to get any more love. You have all the love you need. You come from unconditional love. God did not make junk."

"What you just said may be the most important thing I have to learn," the young man said.

"And perhaps for your president too," smiled the One Minute Manager.

Apologizing To Yourself

After breakfast the One Minute Manager and the young man left to pick up Nana so she could join the family for church. They didn't want her to drive herself in the rainstorm. Annie took Carol and Brad in her car.

As they buckled their seat belts, the young man said to the One Minute Manager, "Annie brought up a very interesting point this morning. She helped me see how I could have contributed to the problem at work by not taking action myself."

"My little Annie! She said something mean like that?" asked the One Minute Manager, pretending to act incredulous.

"Yes. Your little Annie put it so well that I never even once felt like I was on the hot seat."

"Well, she certainly didn't learn *that* from me."

"You're right about that. But thanks to her, I now am beginning to reconcile what happened at work. After all, I was 'going along with the program,' too. Worrying about losing my big salary and benefits. I played along as if nothing bad was happening. Of course, I knew it. I just didn't want to admit it. I, too, crossed the line by looking the other way. By not acting honestly on his behalf, I unconsciously helped my president get into trouble.

"As I told you Friday night, I was afraid to bring him any bad news. Maybe if I had spoken up, things might be different."

"You can't control the outcome of events," the One Minute Manager began, as he pulled the car onto the narrow road where Nana lived, *"but you can control what you think and what you do."*

He continued, "You allowed your self-doubt and fear to drive your behavior. At the very least, *you'd be feeling better today if you had been completely honest with yourself.* Situations like the one at your company don't just happen in a week. It's very probable that many people knew, but no one wanted to 'rock the boat' for fear of angering the boss. What's the president of your company really like? Do you think he has it in him to pull it together?"

The young man answered, "Before all this happened, I had great respect and admiration for him. I owe him a lot, and I'll still be loyal to him, but to answer your question, I don't know. Over the past year or so he's become bitten by what you call false pride. He's been thinking more of himself than he should. As a result, he has become preoccupied with the perks of his position. I wish I had been more helpful to him. I guess I just didn't think I was in a position to do anything."

The One Minute Manager said, "Don't be so hard on yourself. Your boss got caught up in false pride, and self-doubt fueled your fear. You both need to apologize to yourself. Apologize to *yourself* for behavior you're not proud of. Resolve to avoid repeating the behavior. Then repair the damage you've done to yourself and others by behaving differently. That's how you make things better."

"Good advice," said the young man. "Selling it to my president will be interesting."

"And now where does all of this leave you? Are you feeling better or worse than when you first arrived here?"

"I feel much better, thank you. I'm more confident about what I have to do. Learning about the One Minute Apology has made a huge difference."

"And what's the *only* thing that's changed?"

"*Me.* I've changed how I think."

The One Minute Manager challenged him, "Now, are you going to change your behavior?"

The young man wisely said nothing, but began to ask himself what he would do differently.

As the car pulled into Nana's driveway, the rain was coming down hard. The young man leaped out of the car, and ran toward the cottage to get Nana. As he stepped onto the front porch, the door opened and she appeared. He opened his umbrella and carefully escorted Nana to the car.

Self-Respect And The One Minute Apology

As they drove away, the young man said, "You've both helped me to understand the power of apologizing. But *what about the people who haven't received an apology when they feel they deserve one?* Last night in bed I was thinking about how many people are hurt or heartbroken because the person who disappointed them didn't have the courage to admit they were wrong and apologize. What can they do?"

"If something is bothering you and you don't deal with it, what happens to those feelings? Do they stay or go away?" asked the One Minute Manager.

"The bad feelings stay with you," answered the young man.

"Grudges fester and can sometimes immobilize you," said Nana. "Once you deal with what's bothering you, almost like magic, your negative feelings and fears disappear."

"As they say, 'the truth will set you free,' " added the One Minute Manager.

"Now that you mention it," said the young man, "after I deal with pent-up anger or frustration with someone, I always say to myself, 'I'm so glad I got that off my chest.' But I'm not very good at getting rid of residual negative feelings. Any suggestions?"

"It seems to me," said Nana, "you have two choices. First, you can forgive the person for what they did and let the incident pass."

"That's pretty difficult, isn't it?" wondered the young man. "How can you learn to forgive so easily?"

"That's a whole other weekend," replied the One Minute Manager with a smile.

"That's for sure," agreed Nana with a laugh.

The One Minute Manager continued, "Recognize that no one is perfect. And, like your president, many people are too wrapped up in their own problems to consider other people's feelings. By forgiving them you are able to release negative feelings and get on with your life.

"What if I just can't bring myself to forgive without receiving an apology?" asked the young man. "Resentments or negative feelings don't just go away by themselves."

"That leads to your second choice," smiled Nana, "telling that person exactly how you feel."

"O.K. Then I can ask for an apology?"

"Yes," said the One Minute Manager. "However, it's more important for your own sake that you say what he or she did and how it affected you."

The young man said, "Yes, but suppose the person doesn't like my feedback or attacks me for what I say to them?"

"That's what *everyone* fears," said Nana. "But, isn't it worth the risk? Holding on to negative emotions only hurts *you.*"

"Now I'm beginning to understand," agreed the young man.

"When you show the courage to be honest with someone you care about, you show respect for yourself. You're letting the other person know how you want to be treated. You are also letting that person know the importance of the relationship to you, and that you want the relationship to continue and flourish," said the One Minute Manager.

"That's very useful information," said the young man as he took out his journal and wrote down:

✿

When You Honestly Express
Your Feelings
With Someone You Care About
You Show
Respect For Yourself
And The Relationship

✿

"When you express yourself," suggested the One Minute Manager, "begin by making 'I statements,' not 'you statements.' For example, begin by saying '*I would like our relationship to be everything it could be. The one thing that is getting in the way right now is my resentment about . . .*"

"What if I don't get the apology I think I deserve?" asked the young man.

"The main thing, at this point, is to help the person realize he or she did something hurtful to you and get a commitment to change that behavior," said Nana.

"What if that doesn't happen?"

"*If the other person doesn't care enough about your relationship to make some amends after knowing he or she has hurt you, maybe the relationship itself is in question,*" said the One Minute Manager.

"What's really at stake is the relationship—isn't it? That's why it's important to be honest with yourself and the other person," said the young man.

"I couldn't have said it any better," said the One Minute Manager, nodding his approval.

As they were pulling up to the church, Nana said, "I can't wait to hear from our new minister today. The ladies at my club have been talking about him for days. I think we're in for a real treat."

A Chance To Get It Right

Nana was right about the minister. The young man really enjoyed the sermon and was especially moved by his closing story:

"When I was a young boy," began the minister, "my grandmother was an incredible Monopoly player. Whenever the two of us played, she completely wiped me out. By the end of the game, she owned everything—Broadway, Park Place . . . you name it! She would always smile at me and say, 'John, someday you're going to learn how to play the game.'

"One summer, a new kid moved next door to me. It turned out that he was an incredible Monopoly player. We began to play every day, and I really improved! I was thrilled because I knew my grandmother was coming for a visit in September!

"When my grandmother arrived, I ran into the house, gave her a big hug, and said, 'Do you want to play Monopoly?' I'll never forget how her eyes lit up, so I set up the board and we began to play. But this time, I was ready for her. By the end of the game, I had wiped her out! I owned *everything*. It was the greatest day of my life!

"This time, at the end of the game my grandmother smiled and said, 'John, now that you know how to play the game, let me teach you a lesson about life—it all goes back in the box.'

" 'What?' I asked.

" 'Everything you bought, everything you accumulated—at the end of the game, it all goes back into the box.'

"Isn't that the way it is with life?" asked the minister.

"No matter how you push and shove for money, recognition, power, prestige, and possessions, when life is over, everything goes back in the box."

The minister paused, took a few steps toward the congregation, and in a subdued voice continued, "The only thing that you get to keep is your soul. There's where you store who you loved and who loved you. . . ."

On the ride back from the church through the pelting rain, the young man was quiet. The only sound was the swishing of the windshield wipers. In almost a whisper, he said, "That story the minister told at the end of the sermon relates to everything we've talked about this weekend, doesn't it?"

"Yes, it does," the One Minute Manager replied. "Since everything we accumulate in life from our performance and from the opinion of others goes back in the box, we might as well do what is right. The sooner we recognize when our ego gets us off course, the sooner we realize *the only way to repair the damage we have done to ourselves and others is to be honest, admit we were wrong, apologize, and commit to change our behavior.*"

"*That's the beauty of the One Minute Apology—it is the best way I know to make things better for you and the people you care about,*" said Nana.

The three of them rode in silence for the rest of the way.

A Way Of Saying Thank You

When they reached the One Minute Manager's cabin, the storm had gotten much worse. As they hurried inside the young man's cell phone rang. It was the president calling.

The young man looked apprehensively toward the One Minute Manager and left to take the call in his room. He returned in a few minutes.

The Manager asked, "Is everything all right?"

"Yes. At least I think so. The president said he heard about the bad storm on the weather report and he didn't want me to run any unnecessary traveling risks. He'd understand if I was delayed or couldn't make the meeting. And then," the young man said with a big grin from ear to ear, "he said he loved the Lincoln story! He said that it helped him tremendously. He has already shared it with his family too. He plans to read it several more times tonight."

"That's already a good indication that he's in a much better frame of mind to think outside the boundary of his own problems," said the One Minute Manager.

"I hope you're right. His words were considerate and grateful but his tone sounded tired."

"Or emotionally exhausted," added Carol.

"That's entirely possible," said the young man. "If I had stayed in the city, I'd probably sound exactly like that—or worse. I always knew it was important to have time away, but until this weekend I've never been so aware of the benefits of getting a fresh perspective."

Meanwhile Carol took another look outside and suggested they get more weather information. The One Minute Manager asked Brad to listen to the radio for the latest forecast. When he returned Brad reported that the storm would continue for two more days. When the young man heard that, he called the airport.

"It appears that the storm is not going away anytime soon. Flights are being canceled. Is there a train station anywhere in the vicinity?" the young man asked.

"There is," said the One Minute Manager.

The young man called and learned that the last train for the city was leaving in two hours. He made a reservation and called for a taxi. Then he went to his room and quickly packed his things for the trip back home.

When the young man rejoined the family in the living room, he told them that he unfortunately had to leave earlier than planned.

"I think he's leaving because he knows Dad will still brave this weather for a round of golf," kidded Annie.

"O.K. How about if you take a rain check?" Brad asked the young man. Everyone laughed as the rain poured down.

"I'd gladly come back and, yes, even force myself to play golf! In the rain, if necessary," the young man replied, laughing, as he returned to his room to grab his bags.

When the taxi honked, the young man turned to the One Minute Manager and said, "Wish me luck!"

"What you have now is much better than luck. You have knowledge," replied the One Minute Manager. "You now know about the One Minute Apology."

"Better than that, I now know what to do," responded the young man.

"You already knew what to do, deep down. You only needed to be reminded," said the One Minute Manager.

"Well thank you so much for 'reminding' me," said the young man.

The One Minute Manager nodded his acknowledgment and said, *"The way you can thank me is to use the One Minute Apology appropriately and share what you learned with others."*

"I will," promised the young man.

With that the young man hugged each of them and said his good-byes, picked up his bags, and ran through the deluge to the waiting taxi.

On the way to the train station, he felt gratitude for all he had learned. On the train, however, he began to feel apprehensive about what he planned to do the next day.

But his anxiety lessened when he thought about the knowledge he now had to help himself and his boss.

Using his notes from the weekend, he began to write a summary of all that he learned. The young man resolved, *The president may not want to hear what I have to say, but I am no longer attached to the outcome—I'm doing it because it's the right thing to do.*

The young man smiled, pleased that he could now accept his own goodness, regardless of what anyone else thought. He took out his notebook and reread his personal notes on self-appreciation:

You are able to accept yourself when:

- *Your self-worth is not based on your performance or the opinion of others.*

- *When you make a mistake, you are willing to admit it regardless of the outcome.*

- *You don't think less of yourself, you think of yourself less.*

- *You realize it's impossible to achieve enough, gain enough recognition, attain enough power, or own enough things to earn any more love. You are already loved unconditionally.*

The Moment Of Truth

Monday morning, the young man arrived at the office promptly at 7:00 A.M. He had been up most of the night completing a summary of what he had learned for the president. Making his way down the long corridor to the president's suite he thought to himself: *It's so strange to be here on a holiday. It's so quiet, no one would ever guess that everything could break loose tomorrow.*

The young man stood in the doorway of the president's office. There were papers, reports, and charts scattered on his desk and the conference table. It looked like the president had been working all night—maybe even the entire weekend.

The young man entered the room. The president looked up at him in surprise. Then his face broke into a big smile—the smile the young man remembered but hadn't seen for quite a while.

The young man quietly shut the door and sat down.

"I'm glad you had a safe journey and that you're here," said the president, rising and looking directly into the young man's eyes. "At first, I wasn't sure you would return, and if you didn't, I would understand. And thank you again for sending me the Lincoln story."

"I'm glad you found it meaningful."

"The story was more helpful than you might imagine. When it arrived over the fax machine, I was writing my letter of resignation," said the president. "But after I read what Lincoln did, it woke me up and I reconsidered my options. But, I still face a big dilemma."

"I know," said the young man. "That's why I needed to come here this morning. I've had an extraordinary experience these past couple of days and I've come armed with some very powerful ideas that may be of use. I hope you'll agree to hear me out. I have to warn you right now, though, that some of what I'm about to suggest may not be pleasant for you to hear."

"Nothing you can say can possibly be harder to hear than the things I've been telling myself these past few days. I appreciate your forthrightness."

The young man began, "One of the first things I learned this weekend is that *I owe you an apology.* You say you admire my forthrightness, but I haven't been that way lately, with myself or with you. I've been part of the problem, not the solution. I saw things that were wrong but I didn't have the guts to tell you the truth.

"Although you're the president of our company, you're not in this alone. I saw what was going on around here was not right. I feel ashamed that I didn't tell you the truth earlier, but I was afraid of losing your trust or my job. I apologize and ask your forgiveness for failing you. I can assure you it won't happen again."

"Thank you," the president said simply.

"I would like to make a suggestion, and I hope you can take it in the manner it's intended."

The president looked up at him and asked, "What do you recommend?"

"You need to apologize to the board," the young man said confidently.

"I know you're right, but I don't know how to do what Lincoln did," the president responded.

The young man smiled and said, "You're talking to the right person. That's what I learned this weekend. Let me summarize what constitutes an effective apology for me," said the young man.

The president listened intently to the young man for over an hour. When he finished, the president let out a big sigh. "What you have brought to the table today is the missing piece to my thinking. While you have been learning about the One Minute Apology, I've been working on something too, a business plan that I think can turn this negative situation around and get our company back on track. But this great plan is useless unless I rebuild the board's trust in me. I behaved so poorly last Friday. I seriously doubt the board will want to listen to anything I have to say."

The young man was silent for a few moments and then responded, "They will begin to listen if you sincerely apologize. That may be very difficult considering the time and what's at stake, but:

✿

A One Minute Apology
Can Be An Effective Way
To Correct A Mistake
You Have Made
And Restore The Trust Needed
For A Good Relationship

✿

The president looked at his young colleague and said, "I realize now I have been wrong, and I've caused a lot of harm. Would you please stay and coach me through this One Minute Apology?"

"Of course!" replied the young man.

During their discussion, the president asked many questions.

The more they talked the more the young man realized that the president genuinely wanted to learn how to apologize effectively. He was sincere and did not regard this as an expedient way out of his difficult problem. The young man breathed a sigh of relief. He knew that if the president was insincere, it would only make matters worse.

When they finished the president turned to the young man and said, "Between now and tomorrow, I will be thinking about my One Minute Apology to the board. I want to give this very serious thought and make sure I am being honest with myself. Meanwhile, would you consider staying to help our team with the plan for restructuring? Others will be joining us shortly."

"I'd be honored to stay," replied the young man.

"Good. Having you here will be very helpful in planning the events that would need to occur over the next few days and possibly the months to come."

When the department heads arrived, the president began the meeting by saying briefly to the team members, "You're all here with me on your holiday to help with a meeting that wouldn't be necessary if I hadn't made some serious mistakes. Thank you for coming."

Then the president surprised the young man by apologizing to his whole team. He had not expected the president to apologize until he was in front of the board. It was awkward, but the president's sincerity came through. He did his best to let everyone know he was wrong.

The team members looked startled at first, then one of the department heads said, "Well, we came here to do a job, so let's move ahead."

The other team members agreed. After the president's brief but honest opening, they all felt they could speak their minds freely. At times the discussion about the restructuring even became heated and the meeting went well into the night. But, finally, the team had a plan they were all proud to be part of.

The President's One Minute Apology

On Tuesday morning the young man returned to the president's office prior to the board meeting. The president got up and met the young man halfway, and said, "I owe *you* a special apology."

The young man was taken aback as the president continued, "I know you gave up a number of other interesting opportunities at other companies to come and work with me. I let you down in many ways, and regardless, you stayed loyal to me. You are an extraordinary young man. No matter what happens today, I will make sure everyone knows what you have done for me and ultimately tried to do for the company. I promise I won't let you or others down again. I hope I can demonstrate that further in the board meeting in just a few minutes."

"Thank you," the young man replied. "I hope it goes well."

The president smiled with appreciation.

Then the young man and president entered the boardroom together.

After the chairman brought the meeting to order, the president rose to address the board members. He immediately felt the hostility in the room as he walked to the head of the table.

He swallowed hard and began, "By now you are all aware of the gravity of the current situation our company faces. I take full responsibility for my mistakes in judgment that have contributed to the severity of this problem.

"I am ashamed of my actions. You all experienced an example of that behavior last Friday, and for that I am regretful and embarrassed. I wanted to be right. I didn't listen and I didn't seek the kind of information that could have prevented our substantial loss in the last quarter or the problems that lie ahead," he said.

The president had the attention of the board members as the full impact of what he was saying began to sink in.

The president continued, "I recognize how much I have harmed this company, you, and my colleagues, and for that, I apologize. There are things that need to change and that begins with me.

"You have all received a copy of a comprehensive restructuring plan, which I am confident will restore the company to its former preeminent position. Before we discuss the proposed plan, let me say that I am prepared to submit my resignation today. In fact, I have already signed a letter to the board to that effect.

"If, however, you still want me to serve in a leadership role, you and my colleagues have my solemn promise that I will never repeat the kind of poor behavior I exhibited these past months."

As the president concluded his One Minute Apology, the expressions on the board members' faces relaxed. The air of hostility that had pervaded the room earlier began to change. With that, the chairman said, "Please continue."

The president asked the board members to turn to the section of their meeting materials labeled "Restructuring Plan." Then he began to describe in detail the new proposal and plans for its implementation.

When he finished, the room became quiet until the chairman took the floor and requested that the president and the young man leave the room while he and the members of the board met in private.

The president and the young man paced the corridor. The young man spoke first. "You did the right thing regardless of the outcome."

The young man thought he detected the president's eyes begin to mist.

The president replied, "I believe I did too. I hope I get the opportunity to let my actions speak louder than my words."

Thirty minutes later, they were called back and the chairman again took charge of the meeting.

"I speak on behalf of everyone here today. We're very impressed by what you've just told us. We appreciate your apology and accept it. If you follow through on what you say, we will be one hundred percent behind the impressive restructuring plan you've given us this morning."

The chairman then asked the president, "Do you have anything further to say?"

"Yes, I do," responded the president.

The president paused for a few moments, looking toward each of the board members individually, then said, "I intend to work without pay until this current situation is turned around."

The board members looked astounded.

"Furthermore," he continued, "by contract I am protected by generous bonus and severance clauses. But today I relinquish my rights to those rewards. Those benefits and privileges were based on your trust in the person you hired—the person I once was and intend to be again.

"That person warranted and deserved your complete trust and respect. But that person got off track somewhere along the way. I intend to become that man again—but no one in this room should have to subsidize his return. I must do it myself. You can judge when I am that person again."

The room was silent. Then, spontaneously, everyone rose to their feet and applauded.

The president directed his attention to the young man and all the eyes in the room followed his. He said, "Finally, I want you all to know about a very special young man who went to great lengths to help me through this perilous situation . . ."

The young man stopped taking notes of the meeting. Recalling the special moments of the weekend with the One Minute Manager and his family at the lake, he looked upward, and quietly whispered, "Thank you."

At that very moment the young man understood the full impact of the One Minute Manager's parting words to him right before he left the lake:

✻

*The Way To Thank Me
Is To Use The One Minute Apology
And Share What You've Learned
With Others*

✻

Epilogue

That evening the young man sent an email to the One Minute Manager thanking him and his family for their contribution to the successful outcome of the board meeting.

"Without your help," he wrote, "I can only imagine what today would have been like not only for me, but everyone I work with, and especially my president.

"I've written a summary of the One Minute Apology which I value as a reminder of the new direction my life is taking, and also of the special weekend we shared at the lake. You and your family taught me a powerful secret that is literally changing my life."

The young man removed the summary from his wallet to review it again, just as he would do for years to come, whenever he needed to apologize or when sharing what he learned with others:

The One Minute Apology: A Summary

I ask myself the following questions, and answer truthfully:

What mistake did I make?

Did I dismiss another person, their wishes, feelings, or ideas?

Did I take credit when it wasn't due?

Why did I do this?

Was it an impulsive, thoughtless act? Was it calculated? Was it a result of my fear, anger, or frustration? What was my motivation?

How long have I let this go on? Is this the first or repeated time? Is this behavior becoming a pattern in my life?

What is the truth I am not dealing with?

Am I better than this behavior?

Then I do the following:

I Begin My One Minute Apology with *Surrender*

- I am truthful and admit to myself that I've done something wrong and need to make up for it.

- I take full responsibility for my actions and sincerely recognize the need to apologize to anyone I have harmed, regardless of the outcome.

- I have a sense of urgency about apologizing—I act as soon as possible.

- I tell anyone harmed specifically what I did wrong.

- I share how I feel about what I did with those harmed.

I Complete My One Minute Apology with *Integrity*

- I recognize that what I did is inconsistent with who I want to be.

- I reaffirm I am better than my poor behavior and forgive myself.

- I recognize how much I have hurt another person by making amends and demonstrate my commitment not to repeat the act by changing my behavior.

Acknowledgments

We wish to give a praising to many of the people who helped us make this a better book, including:

Margie Blanchard and Nevins McBride, our spouses, who have skillfully and lovingly made our lives almost apology free; Debbie Blanchard Medina and Scott Blanchard; Kim Sauer McBride, Leslie McBride Ege, Robyn McBride Deuber, and Kelly Wright, our children, with whom we have shared many worthwhile apologies over the years and for their insights with our book, and to the continued practice with our grandchildren Kurtis and Kyle Blanchard, Phoebe and Annabel Wright, Carly Ege, and Wylie Deuber; Donna DeGutis and Renee Vincent of the McBride Literary Agency for their publishing professionalism; James Dodson for suggesting N.A.T.O. (Not Attached To Outcome) as a wonderful way to play golf and live life; Dottie Hamilt, who was always there for Ken; Phil Hodges for his encouragement, guidance, and continual help; Jennifer James for what she taught us about the sources of self-esteem; Spencer Johnson, not only for his wonderful foreword, but his wise counsel; Larry Hughes and Pat Golbitz for their early editorial guidance; Robert S. McGee for what we learned about self-worth; John Ortberg for sharing his story of playing Monopoly with his grandmother;

Charlie and Vera Richardson for being examples of living an honest life; the late Carl Sandburg for his wonderful description of Lincoln's apology; our publisher, Michael Morrison, for his leadership; our editor, Henry Ferris, for his editorial brilliance and unflagging support championing our book; Carrie Kania for her fabulous marketing efforts; Kristen Green and Debbie Stier for their phenomenal PR campaign; Jane Friedman for believing in the book from the beginning; Cathy Hemming for cheering us on; and Claire Wachtel, Libby Jordon, and Brenda Segal for their friendship, a good laugh once in a while, enthusiasm, creativity, and boldness throughout the publishing process; Lisa Queen of IMG for her support when this book was merely a proposal and her continued expertise in representing the book to foreign markets; our generous reviewers for their feedback: First and foremost, our focus group at Skaneateles CC—also, Patti Arthur, Trudy Atchinson, Marilynn Boesky, Sheldon Bowles, Lee Bruckman, Jason Cabassi, Jessica Clark, Steve Diamond, Richard Farson, Lawrence Goldberger, Paula Hauer, Jeanne Jones, Tracy Kelleher, Kim Kruckel Batista, Fleur Lawrence, Sangeeta Mehta, Peggy Manoogian, Kathy Park, Carol Randolph, Renee Richardson, David Rozen, Marjorie Shaevitz, Susan Schutz, Susan Scott, Sheldon Siegel, Will Stewart, Jeanne Welch, and Kris Wallace.

Services Available

If this book inspired you to apologize to someone you have wronged and you offered a timely and effective apology, please tell us your story. How did it go? What happened? Did it make your life and the lives of anyone you wronged better? Tell us about it at: oma@oneminuteapology.com.

Ken Blanchard and Margret McBride speak at conventions and to organizations all over the world through the Speakers Bureau at The Ken Blanchard Companies. For additional information on their speaking activities, please contact:

The Ken Blanchard Companies	Margret McBride
125 State Place	PMB 264
Escondido, CA 92029	7660 Fay Ave., Ste. H
1-800-728-6000 or	La Jolla, CA 92037
1-760-489-5005	1-858-270-6600

The Ken Blanchard Companies is a global leader in workplace learning, employee productivity, and leadership effectiveness. Building upon the principles of Ken's books, the company is recognized as a thought leader in leveraging leadership skills and acknowledging the value of people in order to accomplish strategic objectives. The Ken Blanchard Companies not only helps people learn, but also ensures that they cross the bridge from learning to doing. To learn more about The Ken Blanchard Companies, visit the website at www.kenblanchard.com.

"'To err is human, to fess up to it divine,' with apologies to Alexander Pope. McBride and Blanchard offer readers a simple yet effective way to understand and implement emotional healing in the aftermath of life's missteps. They acknowledge that full engagement in personal or business life dictates that miscalculations will occur; but they take this one step further by providing a system to rectify them and resume toward a path of full human functioning."

 —Stephen M. Pfeiffer, Ph.D., executive director of
  the Association for the Advancement of Psychology

"The beauty of *The One Minute Apology* is its simplicity. It's the golden rule expanded to fit every situation, and anyone can use it in their workplace or just to make their lives better."

 —Jeanne Jones, author of the syndicated column
  "Cook It Light"

"*The One Minute Apology* offers timeless lessons on facing reality. The honest apology described in this book is an investment with countless rewards. This simple advice is priceless."

 —Rosanne Badowski, executive assistant to Jack
  Welch and author of *Managing Up*

"To apologize is a sign of strength, a long-neglected art that can change your personal and business relations. Today more than ever it is the missing link in saving corporate America. I am sending my copy to Kenneth Lay!"

 —Noël Riley Fitch, author of *Appetite for Life: The
  Biography of Julia Child* and *Sylvia Beach and the
  Lost Generation*